SMOKIN' MOTORCYCLES

BOB WOODS

Speeding Star
an imprint of
Enslow Publishers, Inc.

Speeding Star, an imprint of Enslow Publishers, Inc. Original edition published as *Hottest Motorcycles* © 2008 by Enslow Publishers, Inc.

Library of Congress Cataloging-in-Publication Data

Woods, Bob.
  Smokin' motorcycles / Bob Woods.
    pages cm. — (Fast wheels!)
  Previously titled: Hottest motorcycles.
  Includes bibliographical references and index.
  Summary: "Learn about the motorcycle's beginning, the chopper phenomenon,
and motorcycle racing"—Provided by publisher.
  ISBN 978-1-62285-085-3 (alk. paper)
  1. Motorcycles, Racing—Juvenile literature. 2. Motorcycles—Performance—Juvenile literature. 3.
  Motorcycle racing—Juvenile literature. I. Title.
  TL440.15.W664 2013
  629.227′5—dc23
                              2012047637

Future Editions
Paperback ISBN: 978-1-62285-086-0
EPUB ISBN: 978-1-62285-088-4
Single-User PDF ISBN: 978-1-62285-089-1
Multi-User PDF ISBN: 978-1-62285-160-7

Printed in the United States of America

062013 Lake Book Manufacturing, Inc., Melrose Park, IL

10 9 8 7 6 5 4 3 2 1

Speeding Star
Box 398, 40 Industrial Road
Berkeley Heights, NJ 07922
USA
www.speedingstar.com

Photo Credits: AP Images/Cal Sport Media, p. 34 (bottom left); AP Images/Chris Pizzello, p. 26; AP Images/ Chris Polk, p. 34 (top right); AP Images/Darron Cummings, p. 1; AP Images/Eranga Jayawardena, p. 34 (top left); AP Images/Jeffrey Phelps, p. 17; AP Images/Kin Cheung, p. 4; AP Images/Marcelo Maragni, p. 9 (bottom); AP Images/Mat Gdowski, p. 3; AP Images/ Morry Gash, pp. 7, 20; AP Images/Petr David Josek, p. 40; AP Images/ PRNewsFoto/Coors Brewing Company, p. 24; AP Images/The Plain Dealer/Beth Skabar, p. 34 (middle); AP Images/Tim Sharp, p. 28; © Corel Corporation, pp. 9 (top and middle), 11, 16, 21, 31, 32, 37, 39; Faiz Zaki/ Shutterstock.com, p. 42; lekkyjustdoit/Shutterstock.com, p. 43; reezuan/Shutterstock.com, p. 19; Watchtheworld/ Shutterstock.com, p. 13.

Cover Photo: AP Images/Darron Cummings.

CONTENTS

**John McGuinness (front) is always battling to be No. 1.
Here, he is neck-and-neck with rival racer Michael Rutter.**

ON THE
FAST TRACK

John McGuinness is about to make history. He is riding a Honda CBR1000RR, one of the hottest superbikes in the world. McGuinness is leading the 2012 Isle of Man Superbike TT motorcycle race. He is racing along at about 180 miles per hour (mph). The force of the air around him is incredible. Slowing down to 40 mph for a tricky left-hand curve, he leans the bike over. McGuinness's left knee nearly scrapes the pavement. His heart beats a little faster, but he gets through the turn with no problem.

The Isle of Man is a small, hilly island in the Irish Sea, halfway between Great Britain and Ireland. Its narrow, twisty roads have hosted hundreds of thrilling, high-speed races. The course is 37 miles long. This race will take McGuinness and the other competitors around the course six times, for a total of nearly 226 miles.

McGuinness speeds up again. The finish line is in sight. No one is going to catch him. He passes under the checkered flag. He has not only won the race, but set a new world record. His average speed is an incredible 128.078 mph! This doesn't break the record, but that's okay because he already owns the record for fastest average speed ever at 131.578 mph. He set that mark in 2009 in a Senior TT race.

RACING ON TWO WHEELS

Humans have always loved to go fast—and then go faster than the other guy or girl. The ultimate goal is to be named the fastest, no matter how we are traveling.

In 1867, Sylvester Howard Roper, an inventor from Massachusetts, bolted a small steam-powered engine to a bicycle. He connected the simple motor to pulleys and belts that turned the bike's back wheel. The motorcycle was born! In 1885, Germany's Gottlieb Daimler figured out how to

William G. Davidson is the grandson of William A. Davidson, one of the founders of Harley-Davidson. He is now the senior vice president of the company.

attach a more powerful gas-powered motor to a bicycle.

By the beginning of the twentieth century, dozens of manufacturers in the United States and Europe were selling motorcycles. In the United States, the big names included Indian, Curtiss, Cyclone, and Harley-Davidson. Popular European bikes included Peugeot, BMW, Moto Guzzi, and Triumph.

It was only natural that motorcycle racing would soon take off. The very earliest races were held on dirt horse-racing tracks. The first official American motorcycle race was at a horse track in Los Angeles in May 1901.

Other speed demons began racing motorcycles up steep dirt hills, along hard sand beaches, down city streets, and around paved tracks. The craziest— and scariest— were board-track motorcycle races held on high-banked, circular speedways made from wooden boards. Specially built board-track bikes reached speeds of 100 mph and more! Their engines leaked oil onto the tracks, which made the

OFF TO THE MOTORCYCLE RACES

A few other examples of AMA races are:

Road races (sometimes called circuit races): Courses are set along public roads or specially built tracks. Competitors ride MotoGP (motorcycle Grand Prix) bikes and superbikes. These are lightweight racers with engines of at least 1000cc.

Motocross: This is the world's most popular—and extreme—type of motorcycle racing. Packs of riders zoom around outdoor dirt tracks filled with challenging hills, jumps, and turns. Its close cousin is Supercross, with dirt tracks built inside stadiums and arenas. Most racers ride 250cc or 450cc motocross bikes.

Endurance: These on- and off-road races usually last for several days and cover very long distances. Special "enduro" bikes are similar to motocross models. Endurance races are run in many different countries. One of the most famous is the Dakar Rally. In 2012, the race began in Mar Del Plata, Argentina, and ended—about 5,214 miles later—in Lima, Peru.

tracks like wooden slip-and-slides. Crashes were common. Imagine the splinters!

Eventually, most of the early motorcycle manufacturers went out of business. Today, Harley-Davidson is the top American company. In Europe, Ducati, Moto Guzzi, Aprilia, and Triumph are the leading brands. Beginning in the 1950s, Japanese companies got into the business. Honda, Yamaha, Suzuki, and Kawasaki have become motorcycle giants. All together, these bike makers keep today's racers and their fans, as well as street riders, revved up. Every year, their designers and engineers crank out lighter, sleeker, more powerful, and ever-faster machines.

RACING AROUND THE WORLD

Like John McGuinness, many of the world's best motorcycle racers have gathered at the Isle of Man TT (Tourist Trophy) races every year since 1907. In the United States, the American Motor-cyclist Association (AMA) sponsors several types of racing events. The AMA is associated with the

Dirt-track racers burst out of the starting gate for a race in the AMA Flat Track Championship series.

International Motorcycling Federation, which organizes races around the world.

The oldest type of AMA racing is flat track—sometimes called dirt track—racing. The AMA began holding flat track races in 1945. Packs of riders, barely inches apart, lean sharply as they steer their machines around oval dirt tracks at speeds over 100 mph. AMA Flat Track Championship races are scheduled from March through October. Many are held on tracks at state fairgrounds in Florida, Illinois, California, and other states.

Rich King rules Harley's Screamin' Eagle Flat Track team. The team is also known as the Wrecking Crew because they usually wreck opponents' hopes of beating them. King rides a black and orange XR 750cc Harley. Between 1980 and 2005, King won 19 AMA Grand National races and was runner-up for the AMA Flat Track Championship three times.

Screamin' Eagle also has a Pro Stock drag-racing team that features specially equipped Harley-Davidson V-Rod models. Drag racing is all about who can go the fastest. Pairs of riders roar straight down a quarter-mile track at blinding

RECORD-BREAKERS

- American Rocky Robinson set the motorcycle land speed record in September 2010 at the famous Bonneville Salt Flats in Utah. Many land speed records for cars and motorcycles have been set on that long, barren stretch of desert. Robinson rode a long bike surrounded by a fiberglass shell, called a "streamliner." It looks more like a bobsled than a motorcycle, and was powered by a 2600cc, 900-horsepower (hp) engine. He reached an amazing average speed of 376.363 mph. He also owns the top land speed record which is over 394 mph!!

- Giacomo Agostini of Italy holds the world record for most World Motorcycle Championship races won in a career, with 122. From 1965 to 1977 he won 68 races in the 500cc class and 54 in the 350cc class. The World Motorcycle Championships are organized by the International Motorcycling Federation.

speeds of nearly 200 mph. Screamin' Eagle's Andrew Hines was the national champion in 2004, 2005, and 2006.

Motorcycle racing can be dangerous, but riders and race organizers have worked together to make the sport safer than ever. The bikes must have special safety equipment. Riders are required to wear protective clothing and full-face crash helmets. Being the fastest is the constant goal, but safety always comes in first.

BORN TO BE WILD

You cannot help but take notice when you hear one rumbling your way. You recognize the deep growl of the engine—it sounds something like *potato, potato, potato!* Then the two-wheeler pulls up. You gaze at the familiar teardrop-shaped gas tank, the V-twin engine underneath it, and all that glistening chrome. You think to yourself, *that Harley-Davidson is one cool machine!*

Motorcyclists—and those who wish they were—have been saying the same thing since 1903. That's the year when four clever guys in Milwaukee put together their very first motorcycles. Brothers William, Walter, and Arthur Davidson, along with William Harley, created one of the most successful companies in U.S. business history.

The Harley-Davidson Fat Boy was a huge success and remains one of America's favorite bikes.

Harley-Davidson is the longtime king of the "cruiser" category of motorcycles. Most cruisers are heavyweight street bikes with engines of 650cc or larger. They are powerful enough to comfortably carry a rider and passenger on an open highway at 70 mph—though on a closed racetrack they can easily go 100 mph or more.

Harley started the cruiser trend way back in 1936 with the Model EL, famously known as the Knucklehead (so-called for large bolts on the

HOG WILD

Harley-Davidson has grown into much more than a giant motorcycle manufacturer. Those Harleys, and the men and women who have ridden them for more than a century, are also part of a legendary "biker" lifestyle. Bikers take pride not only in owning a Hog—a favorite nickname for a Harley—but enjoy the freedom of riding one on the open road, often in large groups. Many bikers wear black leather jackets, blue jeans, leather boots, a bandana, and wrap-around sunglasses—all part of the biker image.

Harley-Davidson has the most loyal following of just about any brand. How loyal? Well, it is not unusual for Harley-Davidson owners to get a tattoo on their body showing the company's famous "Bar & Shield" logo!

engine that look like knuckles on a fist). Harley's current models go by names such as Sportster, Dyna, Touring, Trike, V-Rod, and Softail. Today, most of Harley's cruiser competition comes from the Japanese motorcycle builders, which make lots of Harley look-alikes.

Touring motorcycles are cruisers that are outfitted for long-distance travel. A fairing—a molded fiberglass piece that covers the front of the bike—and a windshield reduce air resistance, and saddlebags hold clothes and gear. These bikes are called full dressers because they are "fully dressed" with touring equipment. Models include the Harley-Davidson Road King and Street Glide and the Honda Gold Wing. Many have CD/MP3 players with surround sound, cruise control, heated grips, navigation systems, and air bags. Because they are so comfortable, these cruisers are the ultimate touring machines.

CRUISER ENGINES

The V-twin engine has been a Harley-Davidson tradition since the company introduced its first

The Honda Gold Wing is a cushy full-dresser designed for long-distance travel.

one in 1909. The V-twin is a two-cylinder motor. The cylinders are set, from front to back, at a 45-degree "V" angle.

Harley engineers have changed and improved the V-twin over the years. The newest version, the Twin Cam 103, is 1,690cc (103 cubic inches) and over 80 hp. Other companies' cruisers have V-twins, as well as different types of two-cylinder engines. There are also three-, four-, and even six-cylinder motorcycle engines, such as those used

STURGIS: WHERE BIKERS FLOCK

Every summer, several hundred thousand bikers return to Sturgis, a small town in the rolling Black Hills of South Dakota. The event began in 1938, when Pappy Hoel, a local motorcycle club member, gathered fellow bikers for a few days of riding and races. The event grew and grew. In the summer of 2000, a record-breaking crowd of more than 633,000 bikers traveled to Sturgis to welcome the new millennium in rip-roaring style.

The bikers park and parade up and down Main Street. They shop for souvenirs at dozens of stores, party at clubs and outdoor concerts, and go on motorcycle rides. Favorite attractions in the area include Mount Rushmore, Devils Tower (in nearby Wyoming), Custer State Park, and the Crazy Horse Memorial.

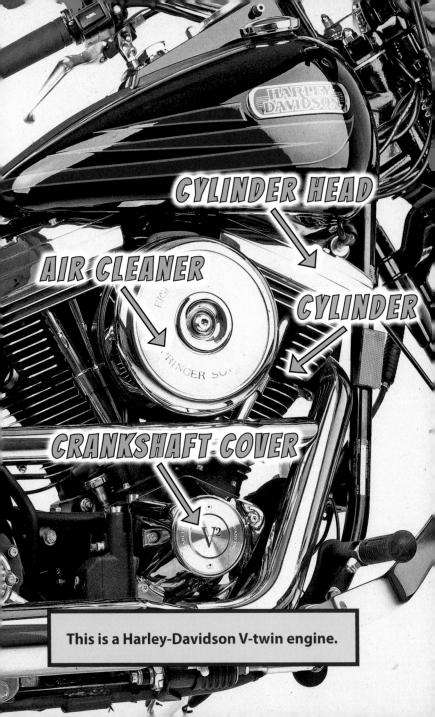

CYLINDER HEAD

AIR CLEANER

CYLINDER

CRANKSHAFT COVER

This is a Harley-Davidson V-twin engine.

on the BMW K 1600 GT and GTL and Honda Gold Wing.

The Japanese manufacturers have introduced their own classic-looking imitations of Harley's V-twin-powered motorcycles. Honda has its Shadow series and 1300 Custom Series. Kawasaki calls it the Vulcan. Suzuki has several Boulevard and V-Strom models. Yamaha has the V-Star, Roadliner, Stratoliner, Raider, Road Star, and Warrior lines.

PERSONALIZED CRUISERS

Every owner loves to make his or her cruiser unique. They add chrome to engine parts, custom mirrors and lights, specially made exhaust pipes, fancy seats and handlebars, and lots of other extras. Motorcycle manufacturers provide thick catalogs that list custom parts and accessories, including clothing, helmets, and safety equipment. Plus, hundreds of independent companies offer even more goodies.

CHOPPER MANIA

Motorcyclists often talk about being independent and not part of the everyday crowd. That might explain why they choose to express themselves with hot-looking cruisers. No two appear quite the same.

The idea of customizing a motorcycle to make it one of a kind is nothing new, but some people take it to the extreme. Their bikes are called choppers. Choppers have become very popular, thanks in part to several celebrity builders, including Arlen Ness, Jesse James, and the father-and-sons team at Orange County Choppers.

Choppers are often built from scratch, either in someone's garage or at a specialty motorcycle shop. For those built from scratch, the process begins by designing and then welding together a custom frame from metal tubing and a gas tank from sheets of unpainted steel. The wheels, fenders (that cover the wheels), front forks (bars that attach the handlebars to the front wheel), handlebars, and other parts either come from a manufacturer or are made by the builder. Engines are also ordered from various manufacturers.

This is a one-of-a-kind chopper was designed by Jesse James for a national contest.

The chopper builder often customizes the engine to make it more powerful. He will probably add lots of extra chrome, too. After all the custom parts are assembled, the final touch is a dazzling paint job.

In the early 1950s, the idea of motorcycle customization was spreading across the country. Some of the bikes were called "bobbers," because parts were bobbed (shortened) or chopped off. By the 1960s, the word "chopper" had become the popular term for a motorcycle whose frame was cut or "chopped" to make the motorcycle longer.

While some owners were adding parts to their cruisers to set them up for touring, others were removing things to make their bikes lighter, faster, and different. They chopped fenders, replaced big lights with smaller ones, and shortened exhaust pipes. They put a skinnier tire on the front or a fatter one on the back. They added "raked," or extended, front forks, high-rise "ape-hanger" handlebars (so-called because with their arms up high, bikers looked a little like apes "hanging"

DISCOVERING CAPTAIN AMERICA

The chopper that actor Peter Fonda rode in *Easy Rider* is better remembered than the so-so movie itself. There were actually two Captain Americas custom-built for the movie. Each was a used 1200cc Harley-Davidson, previously owned by the Los Angeles Police Department.

The bikes were taken apart and rebuilt. The front forks were "raked" to a 45-degree angle. The ape-hanger handlebars were lengthened by 12 inches. The builders covered the chopper's engine, exhaust pipes, and other parts with chrome and painted the gas tank American flag style.

According to the script, one Captain America was destroyed in the movie's final scene. Unfortunately, the other chopper was stolen and most likely sold for parts even before *Easy Rider* hit movie theaters. Many copies of Captain America have since been built and displayed at motorcycle shows.

from the handlebars), and a smaller "peanut" gas tank.

THE CHOPPER CRAZE IS BORN

The 1969 movie *Easy Rider* really revved up interest in choppers. The movie was about two hippies on a cross-country road trip, but the real stars were the awesome choppers they rode. The coolest was a customized Harley known as "Captain America." One look at this red-white-and-blue, star-spangled chopper explains its patriotic name and fame.

After *Easy Rider,* lots of outrageous-looking choppers started rolling out of motorcycle shops and backyard garages. When it came to actual riding, though, some choppers were not the most comfortable. For those without rear shocks, bumps became bumpier. And steering those long front forks at low speeds was difficult. But chopper fans did not care—the bikes looked so cool!

Harley-Davidson and the Japanese motorcycle companies noticed the popularity of choppers. They wanted a piece of the action, too. In the 1980s, more and more motorcycles borrowed

ALL IN THE CHOPPER FAMILY

Paul Teutul, Sr., is one of the best-known and successful chopper builders in the world. In 1999, Teutul and his son Paul, Jr.—they are known as "Senior" and "Junior"—built an amazing chopper called "True Blue" in the basement of their home.

Once people saw True Blue, they wanted more. The Teutuls received so many requests to build similar bikes, that Senior opened Orange County Choppers (OCC) in Montgomery, New York.

Senior's a burly, loud dude. He loves to show off his muscular, tattooed arms, and has a bushy white handlebar mustache. That look, his gruff manner, and the beautiful OCC bikes star in TV's *American Chopper*. After several family tiffs, Junior left OCC, and formed his own bike firm, called Paul Jr. Designs. In each episode, the show highlights the competition between Paul Senior and Paul Junior's shops. They both make one-of-a-kind bikes that can sell for $40,000 or more. One was sold at a charity auction for $250,000!

the chopper look. New cruisers featured higher handlebars, lower seats, and longer forks.

In the 1990s, a new breed of chopper designers entered the biker world. They took the basics of traditional choppers and created a new category of very expensive custom bikes—even though many riders still call them choppers. Well-known designers such as Ness, Dave Perewitz, Roland Sands, Jesse Rooke, Russell Mitchell, Cyril Huze, Randy Simpson, Rick Fairless, and Brian Klock have opened high-tech shops.

Television shows about chopper builders have become very popular. On *American Chopper* and *Biker Build-Off*, customizers jazz up a Harley, Yamaha, Suzuki, or other bike, or build a one-of-a-kind chopper from scratch. Many of these bikes cost at least $25,000—and sometimes much more! That is a pretty steep price to pay. But choppers are pretty sweet rides, and many chopper fans think they are worth it!

MOTOCROSS— EXTREME RACERS

The buzzing sound is like being inside a hornet's nest with the volume pumped to the max. The colorful sight is like a bunch of runaway M&Ms rolling along a bumpy dirt track. The action-packed thrill is like nothing else on two wheels.

WELCOME TO THE EXTREME WORLD OF MOTOCROSS!

Riding a motocross bike is quite different from other types of motorcycling. There are no smooth cruisers, comfortable touring full dressers, speedy superbikes, or cool-looking choppers here. These motorcycles are built for rough, tough stuff, and have riders to match.

Motocross bikes—or dirt bikes, as non-racing models are called—are designed to be light, fast, and sturdy. Whether in a race or on an off-road weekend joy ride, the object is to zip around quickly and safely—even if the rider gets pretty grimy along the way. These bikes have to be strong enough to withstand the constant pounding of bumps and jumps, yet powerful enough to push through loose dirt and sticky mud.

A motocross event is a colorful, noisy experience. It is also loaded with thrills for audiences and riders alike.

CHILL OUT, DUDE!

During the winter months in northern states that get lots of ice and snow, not all motorcycles are kept indoors until the warm weather returns. Some are rolled out onto tracks on frozen lakes and ponds for ice racing. Competitors' motocross-style bikes have special tires with hundreds of long metal studs in them to grip the slippery ice. As this extreme sport became popular outdoors, it moved indoors, too. Since 2004, the AMA has held a series of Xtreme International Ice Racing events on hockey rinks and ice tracks set up in convention centers, sports arenas, and other indoor locations.

The frame of a motocross bike is often made of aluminum, which is lighter than steel but still able to take lots of punishment. It has an excellent suspension. The suspension is made up of the shock absorbers in the front forks, as well as a pair connected to the back of the frame, located beneath the seat. Front and rear disc brakes are smaller than on street bikes, but can stop on a dime—or a clump of dirt. Engine sizes range from 50cc up to 650cc and have one cylinder.

The engine is mounted high to keep it from hitting the ground. The handlebars are straight for steady control on bumps and tight turns in slippery, uneven conditions. To keep weight down, a motocross bike has no lights, speedometer, kickstand, electric starter, or other accessories commonly found on street motorcycles. Short fenders are positioned high above a set of knobby tires.

Because motocross or dirt bikes are not generally ridden on public streets, riders do not need a driver's license. That is why kids can ride an off-road motocross bike. Many communities have special trails and tracks for recreational riding that

X-TREME MOTOCROSS

The Summer X Games, held by ESPN, feature seven different motocross—they call it Moto X—events:

Step Up

Best Trick

Enduro—Riders race through a course of dirt, water, boulders, tractor tires, logs, and wide rocks for a certain amount of laps.

Best Trick—Judges look for the most awesome single aerial trick done off a jump. (Aerial means "in the air.")

Best Whip—Riders show off their ability to "whip" their bikes sideways creatively and pull them back in time to land.

Freestyle

SuperMoto—Twenty riders do about 45 laps around a tricky course that is part dirt and part asphalt and includes jumps and tight turns.

Freestyle—Groups of riders zip around a jump-filled course doing flips, spins, and other stunts.

Step Up—One by one, riders zoom up a tall dirt wall and attempt to fly over a crossbar at least 26 feet above the wall.

Speed and Style—Riders go for speed and quickness around a course while offering tricks off of the jumps set up in the course.

Enduro

are fun and challenging for the whole family. No matter where they go, however, riders should be careful to protect and respect the environment—and always wear safety gear.

MOTOCROSS RACING

Motocross racing was one of the earliest extreme motor sports. The sport traces its history back to England in the 1920s, when off-road racing was called "scrambling." The French built out-door dirt tracks with jumps and called the sport "motocross," a combination of motorcycle and cross-country. The popular abbreviation became MX.

Motocross finally made its way to the United States in the 1960s. In 1971, the AMA started holding motocross races all across the country.

A typical race includes a practice session and two "motos" (a moto is a lap around the course). The combined score of the two motos determines the winner. Today, motocross (along with supercross races, which are held on indoor tracks) is the most popular form of motorcycle racing. Kids as young as four years old can compete—though on smaller bikes unable to go as fast as those for adult racers!

IT'S BETTER TO BE SAFE

There is a wide selection of specially made safety gear just for motocross, whether for racing or just-for-fun riding. Regardless, every motocross rider should have the following gear:

Full-face helmet that meets federal government safety standards for motorcycles

Shatter-resistant face shield or goggles

Boots at least eight inches high

Long-sleeve jersey (shirt) made of a durable, protective material

Full-length pants made of leather or another protective material

Chest and back protector, worn over the jersey

Mouth guard

Safety gloves made from leather or another protective material

Knee and elbow pads

Safety begins with having the right motocross or dirt bike. Be sure it is the right size for the rider, has good tires and brakes, and is kept in tip-top running condition. Beginners should consider taking a riding course, which many motorcycle dealers offer.

The AMA has strict rules for riders and bikes used in its official races. Check with the AMA for details.

This rider is wearing all of the proper gear.

STREET ROCKETS

The rider zips up his leather jacket. He slips on his helmet, tightens the chin strap, and pulls the dark shield down over his face. He climbs onto a red Ducati Diavel AMG and presses the "start" button. The 1198cc, 162-hp engine roars to life.

He pulls in the clutch and presses his foot down on the gear shifter. Even in first gear, the futuristic-looking bike takes off like a rocket on the curvy racetrack. About three seconds later, it is in fourth gear and already going 120 mph. The rider twists the throttle (or accelerator) with his right hand, giving the superbike a bit more gas. Finally, in sixth gear, the Ducati is doing over 180 mph and eating up the twists and turns.

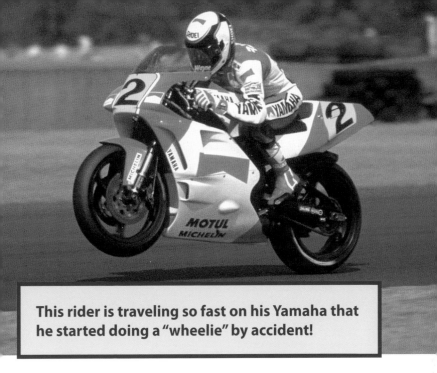

This rider is traveling so fast on his Yamaha that he started doing a "wheelie" by accident!

Ducati motorcycles have been made in Italy since the 1950s. They have always been known for their beautiful design and powerful engines. For decades, hundreds of road races have been won on Ducatis. Just as other major motorcycle manufacturers do, Ducati uses what it learns on the racetrack to make hot sport bikes that are ridden on the street.

Riders of sport bikes have to obey speed limits, but they still like to feel as if they are racing along a closed course. So motorcycle makers give them the best of both worlds with street versions of bikes that have been developed for racing.

Ducati sport bikes sold to the public use engines similar to those on Ducati racing bikes. Other parts of these bikes have been race-tested, too, including electronic displays and lights, brakes, transmission (gears), and suspension (shock absorbers).

Ducati rider Valentino Rossi is whipping around the track as he finishes up another qualifying run in the Czech Republic.

SUPERBIKES

Ducati was not alone in pioneering speedy sport bikes. Britain's Triumph gets credit for starting the superbike category in the summer of 1968 with its three-cylinder Trident. Unlike heavy cruisers, touring bikes, and choppers of that era, the Trident was designed to be a lighter and faster racing-style machine.

That same year, Honda announced its own superbike, the four-cylinder CB750K. It was a huge hit. In 1969, Honda sold about a million of them worldwide—nearly thirty thousand in the United States alone.

Kawasaki was next, with its 900cc, four-cylinder Z1, then the fastest motorcycle on the street. Soon, Yamaha and Suzuki followed with their superbikes. By the end of the 1970s, the four Japanese companies were competing with each other to sell the most sport bikes.

Honda still makes its CB line of sport bikes. All of them have proved themselves on the racetrack and the street. The CBR600RR, for instance, won every single race in the AMA Formula Xtreme

The Kawasaki Ninja ZX-14R is one of the fastest, if not the fastest, bikes that can legally be ridden on the street.

division in 2004 and 2005. And CBs captured every Formula Xtreme Championships from 2004 to 2008. But that is when the division changed its name to the AMA Pro Road Racing Daytona Sportbike division. Honda's bigger and bolder CBR1000RR came out in 2004 which looks like something out of a science-fiction movie.

By 2012, Kawasaki's Z had already become the ZX which had grown up to become the Ninja

ZX-14R. Powered by a 1441cc engine that is bolted to a light aluminum frame, this superbike can reach the last legal speed of 186 mph. It can rocket down a straight quarter-mile stretch in just under ten seconds. However it is measured, this bike is fast!

Suzuki offers about a dozen different sport bikes. At the top of the line is the jaw-dropping

The Hayabusa GSX 1300R is Suzuki's ultimate sport bike. *Hayabusa* is the Japanese word for peregrine falcon, the fastest animal in the world.

Hayabusa GSX1300R, which has a 1340cc engine and reaches the legal limit of 186 mph. It used to be able to exceed speeds of 200 mph! In 2010 and 2011, Suzuki's GSX-R600 won the AMA Daytona Sportbike title. As for Yamaha, its top sport bike is the glitzy 998cc YZF-R1.

Considering today's flashy sport bikes, it is anyone's guess what future ones might look like. It is safe to say, though, that they will all be the fastest things on the road!

CUBIC CENTIMETER (CC)—Unit used to measure motorcycle engine size. The volume of the engine's cylinders is measured using cubic centimeters.

CYLINDER—Space inside an engine that contains a piston, valves, and other moving parts that supply power to the transmission, which turns the rear wheel.

DISC BRAKE—Type of brake that slows or stops a vehicle's wheels. A round disc, made of metal or ceramic, is attached to the wheel. Pads on both sides of the disc press against the wheel. That creates friction on the disc, causing it to slow or stop the wheel.

FAIRING—Molded fiberglass piece that covers the front of a motorcycle.

FENDER—Metal or fiberglass piece that covers part of a wheel of a motorcycle.

FORKS—Metal bars that attach the handlebars to the front wheel of a motorcycle.

FULL DRESSER—A touring motorcycle that is "fully dressed" with such equipment as a fairing, saddlebags, and a rear storage box.

HORSEPOWER (HP)—A measure of engine performance and power. It compares the power created by one horse to what an engine can do. For example, it would take 130 horses working together to create the same power as a 130-hp motorcycle engine.

MOTO—A lap around a motocross racing course.

SHOCK ABSORBER—Spring-like mechanical device that softens a vehicle's ride over rough or bumpy surfaces. Shock absorbers are part of a vehicle's suspension.

SUSPENSION—A vehicle's system of shock absorbers, springs, and other devices that connect to the wheels to assist in steering and ride comfort.

TRANSMISSION—A vehicle's system of gears, powered by the engine, that turn the wheels.

BOOKS

Holter, James. *Dirt-Bike Racers.* Berkeley Heights, N.J.: Enslow Publishers, Inc., 2010.

Smedman, Lisa. *From Boneshakers to Choppers: The Rip-Roaring History of Motorcycles.* Toronto: Annick Press, 2007.

Young, Jeff C. *Motorcycles: The Ins and Outs of Superbikes, Choppers, and Other Motorcycles.* Mankato, Minn.: Crabtree Press, 2010.

INTERNET ADDRESSES

HTTP://WWW.MOTOCROSS.COM

Detailed information about motocross.

HTTP://WWW.MSF-USA.ORG

The Web site of the Motorcycle Safety Foundation (MSF).

HTTP://WWW.AMAPRORACING.COM/RR/ABOUT/

The American Motorcyclist Association (AMA)'s pro racing page.